EULOGIES UNSPOKEN

STORIES OF WORTH

CINDY MCINTYRE

WESTBOW
PRESS®
A DIVISION OF THOMAS NELSON
& ZONDERVAN

Copyright © 2017 Cindy McIntyre.

All rights reserved. No part of this book may be used or reproduced by any means, graphic, electronic, or mechanical, including photocopying, recording, taping or by any information storage retrieval system without the written permission of the author except in the case of brief quotations embodied in critical articles and reviews.

Scripture taken from the King James Version of the Bible.

This book is a work of non-fiction. Unless otherwise noted, the author and the publisher make no explicit guarantees as to the accuracy of the information contained in this book and in some cases, names of people and places have been altered to protect their privacy.

WestBow Press books may be ordered through booksellers or by contacting:

WestBow Press
A Division of Thomas Nelson & Zondervan
1663 Liberty Drive
Bloomington, IN 47403
www.westbowpress.com
1 (866) 928-1240

Because of the dynamic nature of the Internet, any web addresses or links contained in this book may have changed since publication and may no longer be valid. The views expressed in this work are solely those of the author and do not necessarily reflect the views of the publisher, and the publisher hereby disclaims any responsibility for them.

Any people depicted in stock imagery provided by Thinkstock are models, and such images are being used for illustrative purposes only. Certain stock imagery © Thinkstock.

Print information available on the last page.

ISBN: 978-1-9736-0699-4 (sc)
ISBN: 978-1-9736-0698-7 (hc)
ISBN: 978-1-9736-0700-7 (e)

Library of Congress Control Number: 2017917347

WestBow Press rev. date: 11/10/2017

For everything there is a season, and a time for every matter under the heaven: a time to be born, and a time to die; a time to plant, and a time to pluck up what is planted; a time to kill, and a time to heal; a time to break down, and a time to build up; a time to weep, and a time to laugh; a time to mourn, and a time to dance.
—Ecclesiastes 3:1–4 (KJV)

To my parents, with eternal gratitude and love. Now is my time to heal, build up, laugh, dance, and send it out to the world with a prayer that it may help make a difference.

Contents

Chapter 1   Forty-Seven Years of Love 1
Chapter 2   Dear Mom, Happy New Year, 2000 7
Chapter 3   Tangents of Grief 17
Chapter 4   Results—For Nary a Soul 21
Chapter 5   Another Road 25
Chapter 6   A Song for Mother 33
Chapter 7   Christmas in the Ozarks 37
Chapter 8   Storytelling for a Little Girl 49
Chapter 9   Lesson Plans Inspired By You 57
Chapter 10 Storytelling for a Little Boy 65
Chapter 11 Inside the Book of John 71
Chapter 12 Eulogy of Worth 79
Chapter 13 Grief Unscripted 83
Chapter 14 Unexpected Halos 89

Acknowledgments 99
Final Note 103

1

FORTY-SEVEN YEARS OF LOVE

So ought men to love their wives as their own bodies. He that loveth his wife loveth himself.
—Ephesians 5:28 (KJV)

Gazing at my mother, lifeless in her casket: I assume most would consider that moment my biggest hurdle. Within the showroom of coffins, I silently helped my siblings Theresa and Sandi select the midpriced lavender model. I forgot to breathe as Mom's purple church dress was tossed gracefully into the air by its hanger and carefully draped by the funeral director into her casket.

"Oh, how lovely! The varying shades of purple with the white lace of this collar will just really pop," he said, gleaming with pride.

Lovely? No, it was the most horrifying and hollow sight I'd ever beheld. My father could not stand to be there. He was home with the other relatives, but his recent words clung to me with a death grip:

"We've been together for forty-seven years. I don't know what I'm gonna do … every morning she'd say to me, 'Sit down and let's drink some coffee together.' She said that to me for forty-seven years."

My father's weeping was recorded in my memory and was on continuous play. His unsteadiness haunted me. I was already grieving about losing him too. He was ten years older than her, and I always prepared myself that I would lose my father at an early age. Now he was falling apart, and I didn't know how to fix it.

I was also remembering. At the hospital and looking over my mother's struggling body, Dad suppressed his tears, as I did, with false strength, until we finally just sobbed.

Grappling for words, meaning, and hope, he pleaded, "Why, God? I should have been the one. You should have taken me first. God, I know she'll be with you, and we can be together again. Good morning, hon. I love you. I wish I could take you home with me."

Together we were both angered and comforted by God. Too much shock would keep this funeral from being my biggest challenge.

Black. Black shoes, black pantyhose, black underwear, black shirt, black blazer, and a black robotic mood are what I recall. And the impish voice inside me whispering, *Mom, this blazer and shirt only cost me three dollars at the thrift store we like to go to together; you'd be proud of me.* My senses were both dulled and heightened. To my left, I had Dad's pin-striped black suit, and to my right, my brother, John Jay, with his fuzzy sweater pinning me into a temporary comfort. Discarded tissues lined my stuffed pockets, so wet they were disintegrating. Grief causes swollen eyes, runny noses, and body aches, where every muscle is tense and sore; I had flu-like symptoms without any cure. Sorrow brings the lack of sleep, and a brokenhearted spirit breaks down the body. Poinsettias were scattered on the ground, suffocating the perimeter of her casket. All were choreographed in a zigzag dance, signifying the coming of the holidays.

How would each of us make it through the holidays? I knew where she'd been hiding our gifts. They were in my old bedroom—the "mauve room." They were way up in the closet, on the top shelf, or they were disguised in boxes tucked into the corner of that closet, which held all the secrets. One plastic Walmart bag filled with chocolate Santas was propped up near one of the gift boxes. I had caught a glimpse of everything on my recent visit. Mom and I had stretched out across the bed to watch television, and the closet door had been just slightly left open. *Breakfast at Tiffany's* and *Funny Face*—a true Audrey Hepburn movie marathon day. Another movie, although not as classy as a Hepburn movie, seemed tailor-made and produced just to mock me. *Promise Her Anything*—too ironic indeed. Two leading men are fighting for the leading lady's affections, but coincidentally, they had the same names as two recent men in my confusing dating life. Imagine laughing so hard not a sound leaks out, tears are streaming down your cheeks, and you attempt to pull yourself back to reality, but it's just a stutter. Imagine stopping for just a second, and the nonsense meant to be words can barely escape before the giggles repeat. That was our moment. Mom, do you remember? Mom, what am I supposed to do? Mom, my life is in no way a rom-com movie script with cute, minor conflicts and then a happy ending with a sharp one-liner. Mom?

Oh, and then how would my brother-in-law, Larry, make it through the opening of his annual birthday socks? They too were in the secret Christmas closet, just awaiting that day—only a few days away from now. How would Sandi make it through her annual birthday trinket? She was set to receive a very nice nonstick skillet on December 19, 1999. How would we all make it through Mom's birthday? She was supposed to be turning sixty-four. Plus, it was just two days after Christmas. "Love, Cindy" was all that was left to be signed inside Mom's birthday card. Now it just sits, unused, on the file cabinet.

"Precious memories, how they linger …" Okay, I was to hold on to the memories. No problem. Memories are zooming around and drowning me. My mind can't shut any of them down, and I am painstakingly treading the waters of my thoughts while sitting through this funeral. *I'll fly away.* Okay, I was to believe she was in a better place. Just a few more weary days, and then I too will fly away, right? After the cemetery, I suppose life was to go on. It didn't. That was, and remains, my challenge.

Because after, my mother became unviewable and ungraspable—nothing but a mound of dirt, poinsettias, and purple ribbons. I just wanted to climb inside the deep earth and die too. I have never felt so alone. Twenty-nine, single, and now add motherless. Everyone else's life seemed to go back into routines. All the relatives and friends were home juggling daycare, Girl Scouts, evening meals and cleanup, weekly careers, and family weekends. They still had their grief, and I did not belittle their level of hurt. Honestly, however, I envied the love they had to share. Someone heard and saw their tears. Someone reached out and caressed them, held them, kissed them, and made love to them. I lie alone sobbing, feeling labeled "date girl" or the "forever friend," but I'm not kissable, nor loveable, nor even deserving of a sacrificing, committed love of forty-seven years that I was taught to believe in. No, my routine is gone.

2
DEAR MOM, HAPPY NEW YEAR, 2000

> Train up a child in the way he should go; and when he is old, he will not depart from it.
> —Proverbs 22:6 (KJV)

Dear Mom,

I miss you most first thing, every single morning, when I must face the realization, once again, that you are gone. I look into the mirror and hope to find you there, but I only see the reflection of your same blue eyes and the unruly stringlets of hair you left behind. Missing is your spark, spirit, and moxie I so desire and need. Dear God, I pray each day to make it through one whole day without crying so I can stop scurrying off to hide inside the bathroom at work; stop shuffling off inside the bathrooms of restaurants; stop scrambling to get into the dressing rooms while shopping, where I linger in silence to swipe at the tears. I'm yearning to just breathe and to be alive again, Mom. Prayers seem to shift into conversations with you, and I don't know whether you hear me or whether God does. "Stop punishing yourself, and know that I am with God" channels through to me, because I know this is very likely what you would announce to me. But I am human. Right now, I am incompetent. Nor can I be convinced to believe. Sure, I admit: I am a selfish child. What is wrong with wanting and needing my mother?

No more evening rides to nowhere. No more dining out in the park so I wouldn't have to eat alone. No more spying on my latest senseless crush. No more authentic discussions on the soulfulness of my life and love. No more predictions on the greatness of my future. No more preachy mottoes about God's love for me and His great plan for my life. No more. My mother is gone. My best friend is gone. I have returned to my life, but I am lost in aloneness within familiar surroundings.

Sadly, I guess I don't know where to find you, despite my endless efforts at searching. Never have I found you in the memorial plants that I strive to keep alive. Never have I felt your presence while standing near your grave. Never have I gone a day without breaking down.

Now I don't even have the courage to bring flowers to your grave. Aunt Joan says that you understand that I am suffering too much to visit you at the cemetery. From over four hundred miles away, she does her best to listen when I call her to vent about you.

"Your mother's spirit isn't stuck in the grave, and you

can talk to her from anywhere," she attempts to reassure me, Mom. Plus, she told me, "Do not to worry because you gave your mom lots of flowers while she was alive, and that is what is important—caring about someone and loving them while they are still living. Cindy, you did that."

Hearing her voice relay those affirmations to me made me feel as though I was talking directly to you for an instant. So for now, I will devour and savor these words from your sister and have some minor resolution. Someday, though, I hope to come back to your grave with flowers, poems, and stories. Who knows? Maybe one day, I will build up so much courage and strength I will finally write a book and sit in the gazebo not too far from your gravesite and read it to you, Mom.

Swinging at the park one day, feeling like an abandoned child, I was pumping my legs until they ached as much as my heart did. At least in experiencing pain, I would know I was still alive. Higher and higher I flew, wanting to escape, wanting to find peace, wanting, simply, you. Squeak, squeak, squeak—I tried to silence my mind by focusing on the noises of the metal link chains the swings were generating. Childlike motions weren't bringing you back, and they weren't bringing me any closer to a joyful conclusion. Letting my body just dangle, barely hanging on, the swing finally halted.

Surveying the area, I noticed a patch of dandelions. Maybe, to many, they are just annoying weeds, but in that moment, Mom, they made me dig up an interesting viewpoint. People are often like dandelions: unappreciated and misunderstood. Some, even being denied the right to be cultivated and bloom. Catching a glimpse of their sunny disposition, I hinted at a grin. Motivated and inspired, I closed my eyes and recited a poem for you. Mom, I will later write my words down and dedicate them to you:

> Like a dandelion, sunshine scattering the fields, supplying smiles for a season, then quietly fading; turning into seed. Flying away, perhaps one day, seeds will caress my cheeks. Like blown kisses across the distance; fond remembrances for a while.

I assembled a bouquet of the cheery dandelions for you—yellow and radiant, making sure I plucked at the most brilliant ones, because of your unspeakable worth. The juvenile sentiment gave me a fleeting touch of warmth. Unable to withstand going to your grave, I gently placed them at the base of a nearby tree. We had been near this location before, together—during one of our late-night "spins": laughing, talking, and sitting in my car, probably eating ice cream. Maybe you remember?

Among the pretty dandelions were those with the puffy white seeds. Really, though, they were equally as lovely. Each type reminding me of the seasons of life. Holding a white puffy dandelion in my hand, I inhaled deeply. Then, exhaling with all my love, I released the seeds, high into the sky. Standing in awe, I watched as they drifted away. Today, it was my way of saying a prayer for peace, blowing kisses to heaven, from me to you.

So many times I have driven so close to the cemetery but end up parking in the driveway near the gazebo. From a distance, I still know where your name is spelled out. I want to jump out of my car, run to you, and lie down on the hard earth next to your granite stone and tell you about everything you are not here to see and experience. I miss you in the evenings, when it's time to take our spins to nowhere. Do you know, I'm teaching again? But I'm also back in school. Since I have my master's degree, they are still going to let me teach, but I'm going to get officially certified to teach secondary social studies. Psychology, sociology, government, and American history are some of the courses I'm going to instruct. Wish you were here to guide me, and together we could make some creative lesson plans. I guess I'll never finish going to school, but not being able to call you and tell you all those trivial details of my day-to-day happenings in my life makes me feel dead inside. Truly, every moment seems mundane.

Sure miss your support and encouragement. Sometimes, I find it difficult to be my only fan. Insecurity wins over. You are aware of the self-critic I am. So many hopes and doubts are in conflict within me. I miss hearing your voice as you embarrass me, and I try to imagine you calling your best friend, Pearl, to tell her about my latest "A" on a paper. Or eavesdropping as you read it to her. Wish you were still here making copies of my stories and poems and hiding them inside the giant family Bible for me to find. Our fast food outings aren't even on my daily menu anymore.

Mom, I even miss your nosy ways. Say, do you remember when you were snooping around my room, and I caught you? Thanks for caring about what was going on in my life. Something prompted you to worry and wonder, and I understand that now. No need to fret; I had nothing to hide. Besides, when it came to you and me, I was an open book—telling you more of every story than anyone else would ever hear. Hey, Mom—you still were nosy. You knew that I bought the taupe thigh-highs, and it really wigged you out. I explained to you that they were the newer style and pantyhose were on the way out, but you still cringed. You demanded to know where I would wear them. Offering that I planned to wear them with business skirts and dresses, you then wanted to know what type of business I was conducting. So I bought you a matching pair. I miss our banter.

Mom, you also found a few photographs, I guess, while snooping again, or digging through my trash. You were saddened that I would pitch them out, just because someone had hurt my feelings that day. "Don't discard their memory," I believe you said. So you decided to take them and keep them for me. Goofiness, I thought. Well, thanks again, Mom. Forgiveness does happens, and it really is important to hold onto those treasures, to remember the individuals who make up the stories of our life.

Most of all, Mom, I miss my connection to God—the security of knowing someone held me close to heart and, in essence, inside God's hands. Now, I feel like a forsaken and abandoned child who has fallen through the cracks—through God's fingertips.

As an angel, I want to believe you have even more clout with God, but I'm too scared and way too angry to have faith right now, and it's draining my soul. I'm struggling to be comforted by new love and learning to trust its place in my life. I miss hearing the sincere "I love you" from someone who knew me and loved me, without conditions. No one, since you've been gone, has told me that they love me, as you did, even though I know they are trying to show me. How do I fight this burden to be enough love for myself?

Upon waking each morning, I keep hoping for a sign that I truly am going to be all right in my new life. Lack of joy for anything overwhelms me. When I'm happy about my career or the possibility of a real love life, you are the first person I want to tell, to call, to visit, but I don't know how to reach you. I go to the house, and all around are your earthly belongings, but I do not see you, and I am lost.

At night, I pull into the driveway, when Dad still has the porch light on, and your memory is in the spotlight. For a moment, I smile, behind silent, suppressed tears. Easily, I envision you in your paper-thin, green paisley nightgown and nothing else, as you step into center stage with your "What-do-you-think?" smile. Nevertheless, you went for car rides with me, even when you were tired or not well, or for that matter, even when you were not fully dressed for the public eye. Every time I pull into the driveway, I stare at that front porch, and I wish you'd walk out that door, just one more time. God, what I would give for one more time. I am not and probably never will be ready to accept your final bow, or your last "ta-dah" and the curtain to be forever closed upon your front porch stage.

Mom, even the old mauve bedroom seems colorless. Looking around the room, I know that in addition to the movie marathons you and I had here, it also held all my adolescent secrets. Weekends were spent inside this room, with Jackie, my best friend, watching Lorenzo Lamas on his hit show, *Dancing to the Hits*. Too much caffeine from Dr. Pepper had us feeling intoxicated, or maybe that was just Lorenzo's moves mixed with Aqua Net hairspray permeating the air. In 1987, there was such a rainbow of colors in this room—even if it was just a drawer full of "Mother-approved" nylon knee-highs tucked inside those plastic eggs, matching every single outfit I owned. So much color at one time, inside this somewhat empty room. Too much color in one incident, when Jackie and I bought mood lipstick. One cannot begin to name the unfortunate color that lipstick turned on our lips, nor can it name the mood. Jackie would have to wear that color for hours because it wouldn't even rub off—she must have had an allergic reaction or something. Blonde hair, light blue eyes, pale skin, and "Dear God in heaven" lipstick just didn't color coordinate well for my friend that day. You tolerated so much silliness from us.

Although Dad always lets me come over and visit with full access to any room in the house, that made-up bed is now uncomfortable, and there's nothing on that television worth watching anymore. When I come over to visit, Dad often finds me by coming down the hall to the last bedroom door, on the right, and he peeks in at me.

"Take that TV," he offered. "Your mom would have wanted you to have it."

Mom, I had to numbly load it into my car and drive a half-mile away to my apartment. For now, I'm going to put it into my spare bedroom until I can find the wherewithal to pick up the remote, plug it in, and see what Turner Classic Movies has to offer. Perhaps I will find a moment of serenity tomorrow? Repeating the Lord's Prayer, over and over, gives me a tiny bit of peace. *Lord, grant me serenity.*

3

TANGENTS OF GRIEF

> The LORD is nigh unto them that are of a broken heart; and saveth such as be of a contrite spirit.
> —Psalm 34:18 (KJV)

"My Bonnie lies over the ocean, my Bonnie lies over the sea" was drifting upward to me through the heating ducts from the first-floor apartment, and I went frozen. Instantly, I became a child in need of consoling. Tears slid down as my words to the song became "My mommy lies over the ocean, my mommy lies over the sea, my mommy lies over the ocean, so bring back, oh bring back, oh bring back my mommy, to me." On the table, my oatmeal turned to concrete—just a bowl, cold and unsettling. Crying below me had stopped, and I envied that baby who was safely wrapped inside her mother's arms—that warmth that soothes; that heartbeat that calms. My body trembled and shuddered as my arms ached to hide inside my mother's own arms. That insecure and lonely child within me was still hearing her own music.

"How far is heaven? When can I go to see my mommy? She's there, I know. How far is heaven? Let's go tonight; I want my mommy to hold me tight."

Inside my head resides a cameraman who is at constant fast speed. I have not learned to control him. Over and over, in panoramic style he twirls. I can't keep pace between the non-connecting time frames of high school days, childhood moments, and the most current events that have unfolded. My brain goes off on tangents, connecting the dots of all those precious memories. Yes, how they linger. Aunt Mary and Mom had their famous line: "Same yard sale dress, but here's a different belt." Twisting and turning like they were on the catwalk, Mom and Aunt Mary parading their bargains in front of my friends. Embarrassing at first, but then it became an expected ritual we enjoyed.

"Honey, what's my best feature?" Aunt Mary asked, as she stood very poised, hand on her hip, sporting her wide belts and a shade of lipstick that was likely called hot cocoa.

None of us ever knew the right way to answer.

"Your personality, Mary," Mom would say, smiling.

Who would win our next late-night rummy game? We often stayed up till dawn, playing cards. My friends spent nearly every weekend at our house, especially Jackie. Dad called us the "Hardly Able Sisters," since we were hardly able to do one thing without the other. If she and I weren't playing cards with Mom, we were running her errands. Jackie and I were given the grocery list, Mom's car keys, and her trust. Somehow lettuce, which we didn't think looked "salad worthy," became substituted with frozen burritos. Since salad wasn't happening, we didn't purchase the other veggies either, so we had money left over for the canned cheese to smother on top of our Mexican snacks. Mom knew each week we were going to make adjustments to her shopping list, but she sent us anyway. Looking back on the situation now, I realize that my mother found a way for Jackie and me to atone for our somewhat sinful grocery substitutions: Our missions then included taking my grandmother to the store.

4
RESULTS—FOR NARY A SOUL

Cease from anger, and forsake wrath: fret not thyself in any wise to do evil.
—Psalm 37:8 (KJV)

"Where's the cakes? Where's the pies? Where's the fish?" Grandma grumbled as she sped through the grocery store.

We watched as she slammed the loaves of bread into the bottom of the cart and then threw her cakes, pies, and frozen fish right on top, smashing the dough. Painted-on eyebrows in a thick tarry black, a salt-and-pepper wig which was clean but a bit too matted and cocked way too much to the side, a polyester dress in a floral print, and sensible shoes that perhaps a nurse would wear for comfort—this was all five foot and two inches of my grandmother, at least in her outward appearances. Trailing behind her, we still witnessed every hissing sound as she examined items, trying to read prices without accepting any help, flinging her items into the cart at random.

We wanted to laugh but thought we'd hold it all in until we gave Mom a replay of the adventures with her grumpy mother, who liked to inform us that "nary a soul cares about me, and the mailman doesn't even stop by most days."

These were Mabel Sluder's parting words after taking her shopping, bringing her back home, and carrying the groceries inside. Off she would go, to light a cigarette directly from the burner on her gas stove. No thank you. No I love you. Really, nothing very grandmotherly at all. Plus, I knew Mom had called her daily and had been to see her many times that week. "Nary a soul" was just another dramatic lie in the Mabel story.

"David wants shrimps!" This exclamation was just another of the many demands Grandma Sluder left on the answering machine for my mom. Not only were we supposed to drop everything for Grandma, we were supposed to cater to my undiagnosed, nonmedicated, paranoid schizophrenic uncle David. Right then and there, we were supposed to head to Long John Silvers for shrimps. Meanwhile, he liked to ramble on and on about taking the Sluder name, explaining if he took one letter or another and turned it upside down, he could "get results." None of us ever knew what that really meant, nor did we dare ask further questions. The German heritage behind the Sluder name was very intriguing to him. Hitler, he liked to remind us, was German, and he was fascinated with him too.

Within an eight-by-ten oak frame, David drew a portrait of an Indian chief and hung it in a hallway near the bathroom.

I was always amazed at his talent. The detailed feathers in the man's headdress were impeccable. You could see the courage in his eyes. This sketch could have won awards if the artist knew how to interact with the outside world. Oddly, he took steak bones and carved them into what looked like authentic arrowheads, a bizarre talent few likely possess. One day, he was a kind and artistic genius. And the next day, he was turning the family photos backwards on the wall because the people were talking to him, and he wasn't up to listening to their gibberish nonsense. If they didn't stop looking at him and gossiping about him, he was going to kill someone.

Regretfully, his love for the Native American culture would sometimes fixate into rants on wishing he could scalp people or use his arrowheads to injure others. He'd sit and snigger at the table when Mom invited them over for a meal.

"What's so funny, David Sluder?" Mom would demand, and he'd snap out of his episodes.

Mostly, I was always thankful Mom's question to David was rhetorical, because I feared what might have been humoring him.

5

ANOTHER ROAD

Her children rise up, and call her blessed.
—Proverbs 31:28 (KJV)

"I'm not afraid of you, David Sluder; you owe my daughter an apology. Plus, you had better get some medical help," my mom pleaded. I was about eight years old and thought I'd attempt to spend the night with Grandma Sluder, at least just this one time. Like a lot of kids, I got sick. Probably just a homesickness, but I still wanted to go home to my mom. My grandmother was a lot like David; she had her good and bad days. Typically, you could experience the whole range of good to bad emotion, all in one day. Most days she called me "Cindy-Rella," her cute play on the Cinderella angle. Terms of endearment, like "Cindy-Rella," gave me the perception that my grandmother cherished me and liked having me as a granddaughter. Other times, I listened to Mabel Sluder point out each grandchild through the photos on the wall and label each of us: "She's the smart one. She's the pretty one. He's the lazy one. She's the mean one. He's the quiet one." Framed opportunities, filled with the possibilities of love.

"Gramma, are you excited to meet your newest grandbaby?" I asked, since the baby had been born one state away.

"Already met her," she said bluntly. "Met her through that picture they sent me. Up there, on the wall." As she pointed to the photo, cigarette smoke swirled from the corner of her mouth, and her Marlboro dangled from her lip, barely hanging on as she spoke to me. Her wig obtained a tiny speck of singe on the upper right hand side, due to her apathetic gestures of lighting the cigarette by leaning over her gas stove. Stomping and pacing around the floor, she acted as though she had even more thoughts to share.

Unhappily, I learned that she labeled many of her own daughters, my mother included, as "great big ol' fat things." I hadn't even asked any question that would have warranted her to have such a discussion with me.

Why my grandmother didn't just call my mom to come and rescue me that night I wanted to go home, I will never comprehend. However, I will never forget most of that evening's events. No longer was I "Cindy-Rella," because I wanted to leave the ball and go home. Glass slippers would never be waiting for me at my grandmother's house. And if they were there, just hiding by some odd chance, they would never fit my feet. My photos would remain on her walls, framed and labeled. Apparently, I was "the nice one," but that was once upon a time.

Grandma had summoned David to give me a ride home. And he was not in a chauffeuring mood. Why hadn't he just called my mother, if I was such a burden? Tires squealed as he floored the gas pedal just after slamming the car into drive. Turning right, when he should have turned left; I did not know what shortcut he was taking. This was not the way to my house. Cursing and slamming his fists onto the steering wheel, his driving was so fast and erratic. Veering too far over the center line, I worried about the approaching headlights in the distance. We were going to wreck. Too frightened to speak or make any move or sound, I remained stoic. Could I open the door and jump? High speed and locked doors limited my options. Where was he taking me? I didn't challenge him by asking aloud the questions in my mind. On the very edge of our small town, he spun gravel as he whipped the car with a quick left turn into the cemetery.

"You deserve to be here!" he screamed. Through gritted teeth, he pointed out the tombstones. "Freshly dug—easy to bury you, right there."

We were deep inside the local cemetery, where no one would think to look for me. It was night, and no one was else was around. No one was going to find me here. Slamming on the brakes, he looked over at me and smirked, in an evil tone, "You want to die tonight? You ready?"

Shaking my head no, I tried to remain as calm as possible and not cry. Silently, I just prayed. I knew I was on the verge of going to heaven. Faces of my mom, dad, brother, and sisters all came to me. Guess the story of my short life flashed before me, as the saying goes. I didn't dare look in his direction. Survival was my mission, as was avoiding the blackness of his eyes, the slick blackness of his hair, and the devil tattoo. The hair on his forearm could not cover it. "BORN TO RAISE HELL" was the inscription beneath the devil, tattooed in green ink. It shone through. David's veins intertwined with the devil's face, and the devil's forehead was bulged out in anger. Another one of David's spells finally terminated.

After, I really don't remember how I got home safely, away from both David and the devil, but thankfully, it was just a few blocks away. David barely pulled up to our house before I flew out of that car, burst through the door, and was blubbering while trying to explain to my mother that he almost murdered me.

Mom came to my rescue time and time again.

"Hello, I know you must be planning a nice cake for Cindy's graduation and birthday, since she went out of her way to arrange such a nice event for you when you graduated." Mom had relayed those spunky words via telephone to my fiancé, who at the time was in love with someone else and not in party planning mode. I wouldn't even come to know the story about the great cake scheme until I finally built up enough courage to walk away from him.

Painfully, it took me hearing him say, "Getting married would be more of an obligation instead of a true desire." Later that day, after his verbal declaration, I would find his work calendar with highlights in blue and pink. His and hers—all mapped out. Their days off together were in neon yellow with a heart.

"He just might not really be the right one for you." She said this me more than once when I called her, sobbing, from a payphone at two o'clock in the morning because he wasn't home yet. "God, has someone in mind for you. Pray about it. If he's the one, it will get better. If not, accept where God might lead you, Cindy."

Again and again, she tried to calmly convince me. Of course, his version of the story was that he was out with his nursing associates, *networking* for a better future, a future that would benefit us both. When you're in your twenties, you sometimes don't think Mom knows best. She usually does, regardless of any age factors.

Nevertheless, due to her secret phone call, I had a lovely, yet small family get-together. We celebrated both my college graduation and my twenty-sixth birthday. The party included a cake, topped with my favorite: thick buttercream frosted flowers—the only real reason to eat cake. Now, I refer to this as the "guilt cake scheme."

"Another hill; sometimes a mountain; another road with rocks to hurt my feet ." I don't know how many times I heard this song as she showered, did dishes, or sang it as a special song at church. No matter how many times it was, I will never deem it as enough.

Sundays after church, we went to the mall to window shop, and I was allowed to pick and order one of Baskin Robbins 31 flavors, because even in the simplest ways, she encouraged me to be brave, make choices, and try new things. Even as a young child, my mother had faith in me. Other times, we ate lunch at Kentucky Fried Chicken. That's what it was called then. KFC remained a family destination throughout my parents' lifetime. Equally important, she provided me the money to pay for our family bucket of chicken so I would learn how to handle money, compare prices, and read over a menu. As a shy little girl, it was such a blessing to be tenderly empowered, while not even knowing it.

Brown has always been a favorite color of mine, and I know why. As a child, she bought me a set of markers, but when I went to use them, I had no brown. She sat down with me, and we wrote the company a letter.

> To Whom It May Concern:
>
> I bought my daughter, Cindy, a set of markers and when she went to color the bark of a tree, she noticed that your set did not include a brown. She loved all the other colors, but we both think you should include brown in your sets.
>
> Sincerely,
> Nellie McIntyre

Time passed, and one day, she brought in a box from the mailman, addressed to me: Cindy McIntyre, 510 Chestnut Street, Earlville, Illinois, 60518. Tearing into the package with excitement, I would finally get to see what was inside. Markers! Bonuses too—extra browns in the various sizes, both thick and thin. Experiences and life lessons, such as this, taught me to write down and express my issues in an appropriate way and try to resolve conflict as peacefully as possible, with classy diplomacy.

Amateur. That was me. I, the shy, diplomatic girl, who keeps all her emotions entrapped, was not prepared. What solutions did I have in place? None. Memory upon memory keep playing competitions in my mind. All so important. All in the race. All hurdling to a finish line I did not ever want to cross. My composure is not accessible. Grief had me channeling a bit of "Sluder" inside of me, churning, bubbling up, and about to blow. "Results!" Yes, I wanted to take my upside-down life, turn it right-side up, and get some results. Or I wanted to run away and travel down another road, less rocky.

6

A Song for Mother

> I will praise the name of God with a song, and will magnify him with thanksgiving.
> —Psalm 69:30 (KJV)

It's Sunday. My hand is holding hers, but she is unresponsive. "Mom, it's about 9:00 p.m. so I am here for our late night spin." With my eyes shut, I'm blinded to the life-sustaining machines beeping, pumping, and dripping. In this mode, I can psych myself enough to pretend all is going to be all right. "Momma, wake up, open your eyes, scoot over. I want to curl up next to you," cried the little girl inside my broken heart. I wanted her eyes to pop open wide, and I wanted to hear her squeal, "Grandmother, what makes your eyes so big?" Oh, I hated that childhood game, but right then I wanted to play. And I open my eyes and allow the tears of reality to fall. Her eyes remained closed, her limbs limp, but I prayed her heart or soul could see me, hear me, and possible hold me.

She and I were alone inside that hospital room, so I talked so openly: "Mom, I need you. I feel alone. I know you have the power of God within you, and if you have one miracle left within you, then I want you to pull it off, but if you can't this time, please leave the miracle of your strength to go on within me. Please don't stop looking out for me. I will still need the hope that I will lead a fulfilling and purposeful life with a soul mate so that I will not always have to live this life alone. I aspire to be like you. You love unconditionally; you have overcome great obstacles in life, and through it all, you have had so much faith in the Lord."

"Another hill, sometimes a mountain; another road with rocks to hurt my feet." It was my turn to sing for my mother. My fingers trace her forehead as I count every freckle in an attempt to memorize all of her, while I still can. And although I don't easily say I love you without first being prompted, I chant, "I love you, I love you, I love you," and all the while, the cameraman in my head swirls round and round a million pictures.

What gift did you give Jesus this Christmas? This message was displayed on a church billboard. *Why do churches insist on having a fancy neon sign that makes you think, "Jesus buffet, all you can eat"* was my first twisted thought, and then I drove on past alone and shouted, "Jesus, I gave you the greatest earthly gift you ever gave me: my mother!"

Seconds later, my anger turned around as I recalled my mother, Nellie Jeanette McIntyre, believed in the tradition of religion. Every Sunday, as well as many Wednesday nights, I spent my time at church. Mom was usually asked to sing her special. Faith was her only accompaniment, as she required no music. The words to her favorite song went: "Another hill, sometimes a mountain; another road with rocks to hurt my feet, but when He walks along beside me, I can take it, there will be no retreat. I have questioned the loss of a loved one and wondered why it happened to me, but through prayer I have found an answer, it was all quite plain you see … another hill, sometimes a mountain."

My mother believed in the power of prayer, healing, and forgiveness. How much I learned through the testimonies of song. "I can't take a heart that's broken and mend it over anew, but I know a Man who can. I can't cause blind eyes to open or make the lame to walk again, but I know a Man who can."

Well, Mom, I am in need of your Man who can, because I am continually questioning the loss of a loved one.

7
CHRISTMAS IN THE OZARKS

> Whether therefore ye eat, or drink, or whatsoever ye do, do all to the glory of God.
> —1 Corinthians 10:31 (KJV)

Christmas 1999 is one which remains forever etched in my soul. So bittersweet. Opening her gifts—my chocolate Santa would go into my freezer for over a decade before I could part with him. Eating him seemed wrong. But so did hiding him away. I went with the latter choice—keeping him around so I had one final Christmas present from my mother. Times when I want to laugh about Christmases past, I seek out the story I wrote, "Ozark Pioneers of the '80s." This is the type of story that can someday be labeled as a family legacy. It is spoken of often and remembered fondly.

One tradition that seems to remain is our family watching *A Christmas Story* marathon on Christmas Eve, while eating way too much of my sister Theresa's fudge, cookies, and homemade caramels. We exchange gifts and marvel at the gadgets Sandi has chosen for us from one of her late-night Home Shopping Network spending sprees (I can still make my own soda at home with my Soda Stream, Sandi). Then, at some point, someone is bound to bring up the topic: Missouri, 1987, the ice storm survival.

Our personal Christmas story is "Ozark Pioneers of the '80s." Just a goofy little nonfiction piece I wrote in my high school English class to show I understood how to incorporate personification into a story. It was chosen to be published in our school's annual booklet, called *Cool Copies*. Mom was both proud and mortified at some of the secrets I chose to reveal in that story. Pride won out, and she made several copies and sent them out to relatives and close family friends, along with the annual Christmas cards, the following year. Her personal copy remained in her beloved family Bible.

Ozark Pioneers of the '80s

By Cindy McIntyre

Normally I do not listen to the weather reports on the news, but Christmas Eve, 1987, I should have. Perhaps this way I could have been better prepared to live the life of a pioneer with my mischievous niece and nephew. Plus, of course, my loving parents. If only I could have been ready, somehow.

I woke up thinking (dangerous thing to do) that this Christmas would be the most joyful of my life. Well, I opened my eyes ready to view a beautiful day and all I caught sight of were trees bent over kissing the feet of Ms. Suzie Snowfall and Miss Ida Ice Storm. I could hear the tears from the Promise Land falling as they worshipped Sue and Ida. I wanted to scream, "Shut Up!" as the sound of tear drops kept tap-tapping at my bedroom window. A sharp pain, in the deep pit of my stomach was gnawing at me. *"I'm dreaming of a White Christmas,"* did not include all of this nonsense. So, to put a stop to the nonsense I shouted, "Not today, it's Christmas!" Well, do you think they listened? Well, I'm here to tell ya, they didn't. I stumbled out of bed and staggered to the window. Opening my window was a definite mistake. Windy, ice and snow-filled air masses sent echoes of Christmas laughter into my grimaced face. About to give up on this whole holiday ordeal, I counted, instead. "One, two, three, four, five, six, seven." My next decision was to wake up my niece, Lisa.

When I gave her the great weather report, she frowned and rolled back over. She didn't seem to care. I couldn't permit this. Finally, when she sensed my persistence on not allowing her to get into a deep sleep, she hopped out of bed. She had my radio blaring "*Jingle Bells*," while the radio's clock was flashing the bright red numbers 10:05 A.M.

"Let me take a shower first! What can I wear today? I have nothing!" Lisa chattered to the rhythm of Sue and Ida. Hmmm … I could see why she had so much trouble choosing what to wear. Her Guess monogrammed suitcase was stuffed full of every shade of clothing imaginable with the plastic pearl necklaces and hoop earrings to match. Where she found tangerine-peach socks, earrings, and even underwear, I had to wonder to myself. Color coded perfection, at its best. After her stay in my bathroom she finally flung open the restroom door looking as though she were ready to hit a nightclub. But at fourteen years old that was not an option.

I proceeded to take my turn in the shower, but halfway through my non-Christmas tune of "When the Saints Go Marching In," the door was practically torn off the hinges by my hairspray starved niece. Pppssttttttt … is all I heard for about two minutes straight. I could have choked her, but she started choking me first!

"Well, we need a new can of hairspray, Cin," stated Lisa while I listened to the huge thud and clatter as my used-to-be-full can of hairspray was disposed of in my waste basket. Then, as my door was slammed shut, I stood under icicle falls, until the scent of Aqua Net hair starch vanished.

What I saw Lisa doing next, I was not ready to witness. There she was, sitting cross-legged on my bedroom floor, holding a powerful sunlamp to her face, in the midst of an ice storm.

"How long have you been doing that?" I questioned.

"Oh, only a few minutes. Seventeen magazine says sunlight is good for skin and I want a little glow," she reported her story as though she worked as a famous glamour consultant for the magazine.

From behind me, hands covered both my eyes in a "guess who" manner. Of course, I knew it was just Doug, my thirteen-year-old, nephew.

"Get out of here, you creep!" Lisa screeched.

"What are you trying to do, Lisa, fry off your "zittles," Doug cackled.

"I hate you! You're an idiot!" Lisa shouted but stayed composed enough to remain in the beams of the sunlamp.

"I hate you too!" Doug joked, as he run out of the room skipping. It never changed. They were always in a brawl. Ugh, sibling rivalry!

My clock radio was flashing numbers that were near noon. Unfortunately, I could still hear the weather tap-dancing against the house. To top it all off—Sue and Ida made sure they weighed the power lines down so heavily that the electricity throughout the town failed to operate. It's Christmas. It's noonish. It's time to find a way out of this ordeal. I had put up with enough crazy for one day. Searching for the keys to the car was the last thing I wanted to do at my residence that day, but it wasn't. Hurrying to leave, I was thankful we generally celebrate the holiday on Christmas Eve with our family opening gifts and eating, or this day would already be ranking as one of the worst ever.

"Where are you going?" Dad inquired.

"I'm just going to town; anywhere, anyplace, but here. Why?" I begged.

"Sit down and just rest your face. You can't go anywhere because the car has a tree on top of it." Dad informed me in such a matter-of-fact manner. I think now it may have been more out of being in slight shock.

Tic, toc, tic, toc, tic toc. Time ticked on as the house grew darker and darker and somehow felt smaller and smaller too. Chimes of the grandfather clock reminded us of the time. Hour upon hour, after dark. Dong, dong, dong, dong, dong, dong, dong, dong. It's 8 o'clock, we knew. Various scented candles were flickering, thanks to Mom's hard efforts.

Lisa and Doug's bantering sessions and issues were my only source of entertainment. The sunlamp apparently did wonders for Lisa's face, Doug thought, as he told her she looked like a scorched frog. I did have to agree with him. She got a bit steamed when we all chuckled at her. She grabbed the closest candle and located her handheld mirror. Glaring at herself so close into the mirror, she singed her bangs. While she was gawking at herself, I prayed a silent prayer that she wouldn't burst into flames due to that flammable hair-do. Thick, white chunks of Noxzema then clung to Ms. Froggie's face. "Frosty the Snowfrog, had a very fiery face," Doug sang.

In bed that night, at a very ungodly early hour, I was praying to wake up and find I was just having a nightmare. All bundled up, I waited and waited for the Ghost of Christmas past to come and rescue me. Lisa, was in the same room with me. Instead of Aqua Net, I could now smell the Noxzema literally melting off her face! Doug, also felt that he should torment me, so he came flying in to make a belly-flop onto my waterbed. Little did he realize that the temperature had fallen several degrees? So when he made contact with the bed liner he let out a very unnecessary scream. "Why, why, why," I wondered aloud. Doug just laughed and didn't even have the courtesy to answer my questions!

Day two was no better. Since most of our food was perishable, most of it had perished. At the breakfast table I stared at a box of assorted Whitman's chocolates and some of the ham Mom managed to salvage.

"My face hurts and I really need a shower," Lisa whined.

"Yep, you look like a boiled dead frog and you smell like one too," replied Doug.

We all loaded up in the Ford Mustang (we managed to relocate the large tree branch that had fallen over the car). Dad was planning to use that icy wood to keep our wood stove blazing. Once in the car, our destination was my sister, Sandi's house. Pure luxury awaited us. Lights were shining, water was running warm through each faucet. It still looked and smelled like Christmas. She also had "real food." Biscuits and gravy, plus eggs, anyway you liked. My order was for Dad to make me his "yolky" eggs. These are eggs most call over-easy. But, it's a true specialty to know when the yolk is perfect—the white is fully cooked and the yolk has been cooked with the flick of the spatula, dabbling just enough bacon grease across the yolk. Dipping toast easily into my yolky eggs was the goal and my dad always got it right.

Listening to the "Good Neighbor Program," while we ate breakfast together provided us all a good comedy hour. Plus, it was a break from Lisa and Doug's go 'rounds. One man from the Ozarks called the radio station to share his empathy with those of us who were compelled to live as pioneers. He sang to everyone, "Roses are red, violets are blue, and I have electricity, so I hope you do too!" The sense of knowing that "community" was alive and well in 1987, made me so happy and thankful.

Night came and we went back home to live the life of pioneers. Ma cooked fritters on the wood stove and Pa sat listening to off color knock-knock jokes told by little Doug. Pa and Doug sang a special to Ma, "Grandma Got Run Over By a Reindeer." No standing ovation occurred at the ending to the song that went on way too long. In fact, no clapping at all. Just a few small chuckles, with the exception of Ma.

Lisa had snuck off with a candle and her mirror again. We just assumed she was gone slathering on some more Noxzema cream. Locating her was easy. I heard her shuffling through the medicine cabinet for any type of pain relief. Pa had been hiding his liquid vitamin bottle, Geritol. Guess he didn't want us to know he was going to stay strong and young, as long as possible. She offered me a swig. One sniff was about all I could handle. Lisa, while needing some pain killer for her sunburnt face, thought Geritol might help? Sometimes, even just a little "medicine" is still too much. She wound up upchucking through her nose while laughing and crying at the same time. Her face was still burnt and hurting.

Ma and Pa spoke of their childhood days. They lived without electricity; they lived without indoor plumbing at times, they lived without television until the late 1950s, and sometimes they lived without a family vehicle so they walked in all sorts of weather. Storytelling was continuing on and on. In the most loving, sixteen-year-old way, I started begging Pa to teach me how to parallel park in his Dodge-covered wagon pulled by the dinosaurs in the morning.

It was going to be Ma's birthday in the morning. Daybreak came and I was wanting it to be special for her. "Happy Birthday, Ma!" I exclaimed. She glared at me and in a snarky tone said, "Yeah, you all sure have made it a happy one!"

Sandi's house became a refuge for me to flee from the rest of the pioneer clan. But, they followed me in the Dodge-covered wagon and those dinosaurs were racing. Even after pleading to stay with Sandi, I was always being told to head on back to the pioneering cave. It was becoming a blackened dungeon!

We were all hungry and out of Ma's special fritter ingredients (A.K.A.—frozen burritos). Plus, there was no more Whitman's chocolates, ham, and the Geritol had been re-hidden too.

Pa made an announcement, "We are going to order Domino's Pizza until we get some power or until I turn into a pizza!"

Like a miracle, the sky lit up in blue flames and Dad squalled, "Praise the Lord we are getting some lights!" Nope, it was just another transformer blowing. We all lounged around in the faint glow of light with our stringy cheese pizza. Laughing, we all talked about what terrible pioneers we really were. This crazy holiday adventure was becoming absurdly fun! Mom had us playing Rummy in the floor near the wood stove and scented candles. It started smelling like Christmas again—pine and cinnamon.

Guess what? Finally, the next day, we had electricity. No more Domino's Pizza, candlelight, woodstove fritters, Ma and Pa storytelling, or sunlamps. Yet, what each of the "Ozark Pioneer's" wouldn't give to experience another pioneer holiday season, unprepared and still together.

8

STORYTELLING FOR A LITTLE GIRL

For if ye forgive men their trespasses, your heavenly Father will also forgive you.
—Matthew 6:14 (KJV)

Dear Diary,

It's September 30, 1993. I watched a movie today that I could really relate to. The Lord surely did bless me while I watched. It brought back so many childhood memories of depression and loneliness. You see, when I was only six years old my mother had a complete nervous breakdown. At the time I had a three-week-old baby brother. My father was an alcoholic and a woman chaser. There was no one to care for us kids; there were five of us at the time. The oldest was nine-year-old Frank. He was my mother's favorite. Maybe it was because he was from her previous marriage, and she and my father weren't very happy, so she took her anger out on "his children."

I recall waking up at 3 a.m. to hear my mom and dad fighting. "I'll take Mary. She's the only one I want," my dad screamed. "Well, I'll just take Frank," my mother yelled. No one wanted the other three, including me. At this time, my mom was still pregnant but was about to have my baby brother, David. After this fight, my drunken father disappeared for days and was likely gone with another woman.

For the next three days and nights, we had nothing to eat but hard-boiled eggs, which my brothers and I walked nearly a mile to beg from a neighbor. Nights were so cold. We had little heat in our house. We were so poor we had to wear our coats to bed and cover up with anything extra we could find. Dad worked in the shipyards in Illinois during 1941 and 1942. It was the time of World War II. He actually made a decent wage but would spend his earnings in the bars and on women for sexual favors. On the fourth day that my father was gone, it was during a thunderstorm, and Mom left all us kids at home, except for Frank, and walked over ten miles looking for my dad. She had torn her clothes off her body and covered Frank up to keep him warm and dry. My mother was still pregnant and could have had David at any time. She returned home that night without finding my father. That night she drank poison in an effort to kill herself and her baby. Instead, it made her so sick she threw up all over our house, all night long.

About the time the sun came up, my dad finally came home. She was still so sick and angry. In her hand was a lit kerosene lamp, and she tried to dash it in his face as he walked through the door. He was so scared I think it sobered him up immediately. It didn't change his behavior, though, and she just went deeper into mental illness.

With a wild look in her eye, one evening, she stood in front of the wood stove and literally pulled her hair out of her head and threw every strand into the fire and just watched it burn. She was unaware of pain she was inflicting upon herself or her children. Her abuse would continue, but toward her sons and daughters. I pulled her off my brother, David, when he was just a small baby. She had her hands around his neck and was ready to strangle him to death. In saving his life, she tried to take mine. She grabbed the iron poker near the wood stove and knocked me in the head. My head likely needed stitches that I would never get. Scars, both physical and emotional, still remain. I wanted to go to school so bad. Mom would make me stay home and take care of the kids while she tried tracking down my father. If I did go to school and bring home books, she would slap my face and burn any traces of my education, books and all, into the fire. One summer, I worked for a nearby neighbor babysitting, and for the first time in my life, I had money for school clothes. She called me a whore and burned those too. I just remember always thinking, what can I do? I was often so afraid that words would never come. We didn't live in the age of child advocacy programs or foster homes, because if so, I would have been removed from that house, along with all my brothers and sisters.

My grandmother came from Kentucky to help and stay with us. By this time, the rage was over, but my mother took to the bed for over three weeks, and during that time, she didn't even know her name, her children, or husband. My grandmother prayed and called all Christians she knew to pray too. Mom did come around some, but she would never be complete or happy her entire life. And I will learn that no matter what I do in life to win her love, it will never ever happen.

Three days in a row, before my dad died, I had the opportunity to witness to him. At the age of sixty-two, he died of a massive heart attack. I prayed to God for a sign to know that my father had accepted God and he was in heaven. Early morning, on the day after my dad died, the sun was coming up, and far off, it was as though it was coming right out of the Illinois River. It rose so peacefully above the bridge. My dad was in front of the sun, like a quick vapor. I felt as though I was clothed in the Holy Ghost. I've always felt as though this peace from God was saying, "I am in heaven."

Mom never cared to learn to drive or read and write. She was basically illiterate. After his death, her abuse was much more in the form of emotional abuse through manipulation. She used David his whole life. My mom is now seventy-eight years old, and David still lives at home with her. They both are in need of God but will not go to church. My mother claims she was pregnant seventeen times but was able to cause herself to have miscarriages in eleven of those cases. She doesn't believe in God's love and forgiveness for her many sins. David is now fifty-two years old. He survived her miscarriage and suicide attempt and her attempt to strangle him. Now, she just strangles him with the right to live a grown man's life. Her abuse on him has had a great impact on his mental state. He has actually threatened to kill her for giving birth to him.

One day, he said, "I wish Hitler would have come to the United States and blown a hole clean through your stomach and killed me!"

Sometimes I worry he's possessed by the devil. In fact, he claims that the devil tells him to do things. He was pulled over for driving down the interstate backwards, because "Satan told me to," he giggled. Thank God no one was hurt, and they are seeking treatment for him. These two have really scarred my heart.

I am a Christian. My four children have been raised in church and all have been baptized. I pray for them and their mates daily. I pray to forget my childhood. Or I search every day while I pray for just a small pleasant thing that could have happened to me as a child. What was worth remembering? My one real peace is in serving the Lord. I know this very well.

Now, I am disabled, and so is my husband. I've had a mini stroke and a heart attack. During a miscarriage, I nearly hemorrhaged to death. In fact, I could hear my funeral being preached. "Spring time in Glory" was being sung:

> Always springtime in Glory
> Where the flowers are blooming rich and rare (so rich and rare).
> Where the happy angels are singing,
> Bells of Glory are ringing,
> It is springtime forever there.

I saw the gardens of place I think must have been heaven. These flowers were beyond anyone's imagination. As I walked through this garden, I was fully content. The doctor said I escaped death by just minutes.

God, you must have saved me for something I've yet to do.

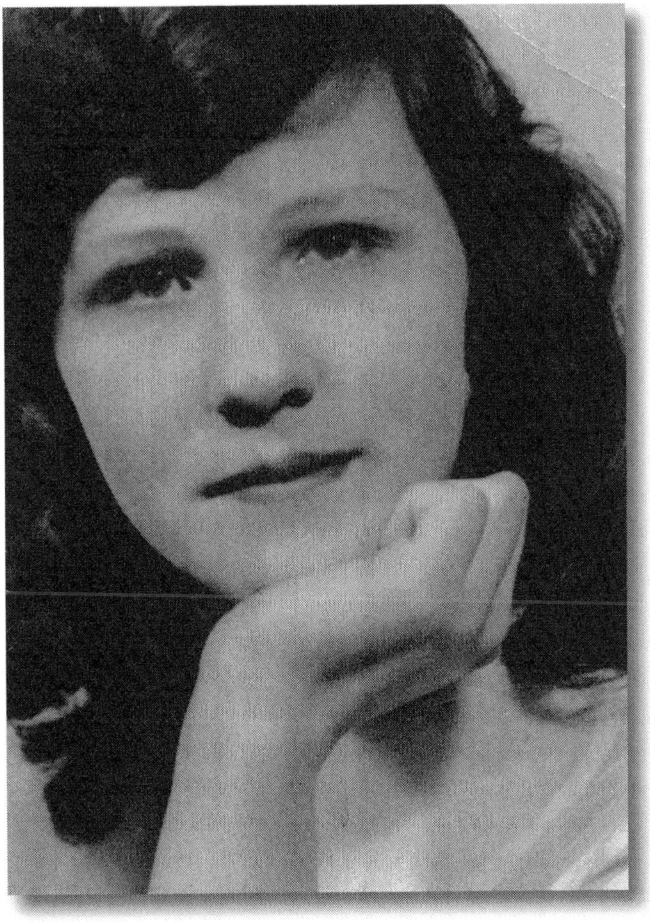

9
Lesson Plans Inspired By You

> Honour thy father and thy mother.
> —Exodus 20:12 (KJV)

Mom, I sat down today and wanted to read and reread every page of your diary that I found after you died. It's been tucked away in my console table, hidden in the drawer with my favorite scented candles and wax warmers. Fall was your favorite season, so you would especially like the apple cinnamon. Your voice came through to me, and I wanted so much to be a time traveler and go back to your childhood and remove you from your painful life. You have to know how remarkable you are, Mom. Being able to rise above a life of neglect and abuse and stop that cycle is a story that should be shared in hopes that others learn from you. How I wish you would have had the loving mother and father you so deserved. Thank you for becoming the mother to me that you always wanted for yourself. What do I do with these profound words? How do I honor your life and your memories in a way that benefits others? For now, I will write them down.

Through my teaching of at-risk students, I will attempt to touch the hearts of those who have been through many of your own emotional turmoil. During psychology class, I created a lesson plan about nature versus nurture. My goal is to have students examine their lives in a nature-versus-nurture context. My wish is for them to consider how to rise above issues and learn how to turn negative issues into positive ones. You are my driving force, Mom and Dad. This is the story I share with them, and then, in turn, they are so open to sharing with me:

My dad was nearly forty-six and my mom thirty-six when I was born. This is considered a bit late in life for childrearing, especially in 1970. I have an older brother, John, who is seventeen years older than me. I don't remember growing up with him in the house. My older sister, Theresa, is sixteen years older than me. She also was not in the house, but she had children young in life, and I was an aunt at the age of two years old. Sadly, Lori died of SIDS when I was three. This was my first experience with loss; it affected my connections and confused me. My sister Sandi is six years older than me, and we did grow up together. She and I had a sibling rivalry. I often accused her of being a princess because I had overheard my mom say Sandi was a "miracle" baby (she was referring to having had previous miscarriages and then being able to have her). Then I heard, "Cindy was a surprise." I took "surprise" to mean not wanted, and this cut me deeply. I remember having my weird concerns that Sandi was loved way more than me, and I wrote poems to show my pain. *Princess Sandi, will I ever wear your crown? Will I ever walk in your royal kingdom?*

I was the baby of the family, but not a very typical one. My nieces and nephews were more like brothers and sisters to me and very close in age. As I got older, I was very close to my mother before her death, and for that I will forever be thankful.

Then I was my father's main caregiver for eighteen years (all the years following my mom's death). Daily, I helped him with cooking, cleaning, and paying bills, and as his health declined, I drove him to the store and managed his medicines and medical appointments.

Generally, the baby of the family doesn't do this, the older one does, but my brother lives in a different state (Illinois). My sisters were both married, with children, when Mom died, so I attempted to fill her spot for Dad, and cover up the void and emptiness. Instead of fitting the picture of the baby of the family, I think my personality within my family is that of the oldest child or an only child. Sometimes, my perception is that I just don't fit into any category. I am a bit awkward.

As far as nature versus nurture goes, I was raised (nurtured) by hard-working factory parents. My dad worked nights, and my mom worked days. This allowed her to stay home with us at night, and my dad could be home for us in the mornings. He was from a different generation where men and women had stereotypical roles (women do all cooking, cleaning, child care), but my dad was a Renaissance man. For breakfast, he cooked me yolky eggs (which most people know as over easy); he brushed my hair; he washed dishes and did laundry. I saw him run the vacuum cleaner and even start dinner so my mom, who worked all day, would have food to eat. She then took over and made sure we had food for dinner and picked up where my dad left off. It was a family of teamwork, I was raised in. No one was labeled or assigned a duty based on their gender.

I was raised to be kind to animals, children, and old people. My mom wanted me at church every time the doors were open. Her nurturing was very rooted in her Christian faith. My mom wanted me to seize opportunities in life: travel, education, and careers. She was likely my biggest fan and always full of encouragement. I remember her making sure I had access to magazines and books. *Highlights,* a magazine for children, was something she subscribed to on my behalf. I looked forward to reading it each month and doing all the activities. She made sure I had a library card, and because of this, I think I have always loved to read, write, and learn. Creativity was something she really fostered in me.

Due to my parents being good providers, I think I have a good work ethic. I have worked at the same career, in teaching, for eighteen years. I still have a sense of right and wrong and the beliefs that my mother so wanted for me. She had to rise above the cycle of emotional and physical abuse from her mother and alcoholism of her father during her lifetime. She chose not to pass on these behaviors.

My father's cross to bear was poverty. He came from a very kind, loving family, but they were very poor. He was brought up during the Great Depression (1930s) and even depended on local grocery store dumpsters for food. Because of this, he taught me to be kind and giving to others who are hungry, poor, and in need of life's very basics, such as clothing. Bullying is something else he suffered through as a child, so he had taught me to use my words wisely.

I observed my dad shower my mother with respect and love. This is what I want for myself in a husband. Some compromises in life, one should *not* make. Choosing a mate for life is one of them. When I am alone, I am still in good company; that became my motto (feel free to adopt it). We cannot choose our parents (I thank God, I got lucky), but we can choose who to love. I am glad I waited for James. Prayers do get answered, even if they are not on our wishful timeline. Timing and patience can be one of the toughest parts about life. "Worth the wait" is a saying that holds true, in my case. We did not even meet each other until our thirties. He embodies so very much of my dad's personality: loyalty, sense of humor, spirituality, work ethic, and a deep mutual love and respect for me.

During my caregiving years with my dad, James was my rock. He supported me through the entire process. He was very attentive. For instance, he knew my dad wore a size small shirt and a size 8.5 tennis shoe; he knew he preferred homegrown tomatoes or those on the vine, and he knew he liked white bread with butter at every meal. Many times, James made these very purchases for my dad, without ever being asked to do so. Plus, he did this knowing Dad would never have the means to repay him. Perhaps one of the kindest acts of love I have witnessed from James is the donation of a burial suit for my father. He is savvy and recognized my father would love the colors and patterns he had picked out for him.

Still, he continued to give with a cheerful and humble heart, while never asking for any accolades. That is a man of character. My dad knew that too. Every holiday, James mailed my dad a greeting card, writing it as though it was from one of his cats, Boots, and later, Peanut. After Dad's passing, I located every one of those cards he had treasured receiving.

As James was walking out the door to leave, Dad would always say sincerely, "God thanks you, and I thank you too."

Because of men like my dad and James, I am aware of how blessed I am to know the meaning of love and nurturing.

Nature versus nurture? In my mom's case, I just don't have an answer. Wish she could have been given the opportunity to be educated. For someone who just had an eighth grade education, she was the wisest lady I ever knew, especially when it came to people skills and being emotionally intelligent.

The testimony of her life, rising above the difficulties of an abusive mother and an alcoholic father, has the potential to change the lives of others. Choices for leading a positive life can be made, no matter what one has had to endure.

10

STORYTELLING FOR A LITTLE BOY

For I am poor and needy, and my heart is wounded within me.
—Psalm 109:22 (KJV)

Storytelling: A Celebration of Life. Today, I watched this very short film for the second time. Although it lasted just about three minutes, it was perhaps one of the most profound movies I have ever seen. It was a silent film taking me back as far as the late 1920s, the Great Depression era. Starring in the show was this little boy dressed in what appeared to be nothing more than an old flour sack sewn into an overall shorts romper. An old rickety porch was the setting. He was just sitting there with his legs crossed and his dirty little feet exposed. Likely, he was only two or three at the time. A sweet but haunting sadness was in his eyes. Was he hurting? Was he hungry? Was he all alone? Someone captured this image of him, so I knew he wasn't alone. History books are filled with similar photographs in the chapters about the Industrial Revolution and the Great Depression, children of poverty: barefoot, dirty faced, hungry, and longing. Although this was a silent movie, music filled the emptiness in the background. Randy Travis seemed to perform a personal melody for this film with the lyrics to his song, "I Thought He Walked on Water":

> And although his wings, they were never seen
> I thought that he walked on water …
> And he was ninety years old and I loved him and he loved me
> And lord, I cried the day he died
> 'Cause I thought that he walked on water.

I watch on as this little boy grows up. Beyond the images and the background music is where the real depth of the story lies. There we find the unspoken truths.

"Ragamuffin, ragamuffin, ragamuffin" is the tune I hear. Bullying is not a new concept, and going to school to face it daily causes great social anxiety for many students. Children danced around this boy singing, "Ragamuffin" to the tune of "Ring around the Rosy." He was born into a family of love, but not a family of wealth. Poverty can have a lifetime of expense on the heart of child suffering through the process. Kids often don't grow to hate school because of the academic process, but because of the taunting social experiments that go on behind the scenes. Recess, a time of "play," can be brutal, even in the 1930s. Funny how most of our early childhood memories can be recalled, even on our 90th birthday, because the names of those who hurt us scar us that much. Those who help us also impact us. An Italian family who owned a grocery store gave this little boy and his family food that was not suitable to sell to the public, but it was still edible. Sometimes, hunger allows for little choice. Food was left near the dumpster, slightly hidden, but placed just right for ease in pickup.

Model T Ford cars were also in the movie. Here, in the car scene, we see this boy dressed in denim overalls; his hair is a mass of blond curls. He's surrounded by his siblings: two sisters and three brothers. Front and center is his stance with his proud parents behind him. Dressed in work attire, the father must make enough now to afford the Model T with his earnings from the shipyards. World War II ushered in work for those on the home front. Still, it would not be easy for this big family, with one income, to be able to provide shelter, food, and clothing. So this boy will gladly give up going to high school and join the other men in his family inside the shipyards to help support his family. Some of his check will go to purchase a new leather jacket and dark denim jeans; the hem will be perfect, just above the tops of his shoes. He will insist for the rest of his life to wear dark denim jeans, hemmed to just the tops of his shoes, because faded jeans that are too long will make him look like a ragamuffin.

By the 1950s, one can't really call him a boy anymore. In

fact, he now resembles someone more like "the Fonz" from *Happy Days*: hair slicked back and slightly piled up, crisp white T-shirt, black leather jacket, and dark denim jeans that go just to the top of his shoes. Frank, his best friend from work, insists that he come over to his family's house after work. While dining at Frank's, he witnesses Mabel Sluder, Frank's mother, speak to her children with such hate. When she slaps the face of her daughter, Nellie, for standing in her way, he speaks up for her. No one remembers the words that were spoken, but the impact remained. From that day on, he vowed to visit Frank often after work.

    Nellie and this man become husband and wife. First, they had a son they would name after his father, but he would most often be lovingly known as "Bugsy." Then, they had a little girl he would nickname "Binky." Local newspapers were also intrigued by this baby, who made her appearance on Easter Sunday. Devotion, admiration, and fascination were written all over this man's face as he poured the mother of his child a cup of coffee. His eyes were glued onto her. His wife, in years to come, will make him a thermos full of coffee to take to work instead of buying coffee. Because he will jingle down past the keys in his pockets to find the last bit of change to ensure Binky has the $2 she needs for the junior high dance.

    Miraculously, they had another daughter nearly ten years after so much struggle. He really did love this lady he saved from abuse. He stood by her through numerous miscarriages and illnesses.

EULOGIES UNSPOKEN

This man, at the age of almost forty-six, finds out he's about to be a father again, and his wife is thirty-six, and in 1970, that is rare and dangerous. Childbearing years are usually over. Surprise, they have one final child, a daughter nearly six years after their miracle baby. The baby grows up, too, in this video. She's often the one running the camera in many later scenes. Brokenhearted after losing his wife, this youngest daughter does her best to take him on many adventures, such as stopping at every roadside farmer's market in search of tomatoes. Floundering together through their grief over losing her, they did their best to restore each other. Outings for ice cream sundaes were to signal in the start of summer vacation, when his youngest daughter is free from work and can go for more rides.

Healing, but not ready to open his home to another cat, his youngest daughter takes him to the local humane society. She admires him and captures him in photographs as he reaches into the various cages to console and love. One cat even chooses to dance on his shoulders in hopes of finding a forever home. Peanut, his cat, comes into his life. Boots, his cat of thirteen years, was allowed to bear-hug him. It took him a while to accept a new style of love since Peanut liked to sit on his leg and curl up. Through his laughter and smiles, we see love was allowed to seep slowly back into his life.

All of them grow up so fast in this three-minute film. He even walks his second daughter down the aisle at her wedding. Not the first time he's stood by this daughter for a special occasion. While Nellie was in the hospital healing from a surgery, he took his daughter shopping to help pick out a homecoming dress. Storytelling continues on, with the quiet smiling faces of children and grandchildren.

Hardworking factory employees who have gone from poverty and abuse to create a normal and yet extraordinary life, filled with a stable home, food, clothing, children, grandchildren, great-grandchildren, and even great-great-grandchildren. They are all an important part of this little movie known as *Storytelling: A Celebration of Life*.

In the last scene, he's offering a final toast, with a slight tip of his cup from KFC. It's as though he's saying, "Cheers," which is so fitting because fried chicken breast, "smashed" potatoes and gravy, and biscuits with extra side of biscuits was a big part of his routine. Maybe the final scene should have been him blowing out the numbers "90" on his last birthday cake? Even better, the movie, *Storytelling*, should have gone on much longer. Ninety chapters is a long life, which still seemed to be cut too short. Much remains unspoken. This man, who was in every chapter of my almost forty-seven chapters of life and who I thought walked on water, was the inspiration for my very first words: Da-da. John McIntyre was my dad, and I was his baby.

11

Inside the Book of John

Let not your heart be troubled: ye believe in God, believe also in me.

—John 14:1 (KJV)

Sitting down, I long to organize my thoughts, soothe my heart, and sift through my family treasures still hidden inside each of the thick family Bibles. Dad had placed Mom's purple memorial ribbon with the word "wife" written in golden glitter inside the book of John. Seems so fitting to me that he had selected that book of the Bible because it placed her close to him, if only in the essence of the name, John. I understood how grief makes choices for you that others would never fully grasp, unless they too had suffered through the process. Remnants of glitter had made their way onto Mom's memorial program, just behind the ribbon. How is a person's whole life supposed to come down to a couple of folded pages? Seems the unspoken portions of a eulogy is where the real stories reside.

Mother's Day cards from all four children have also been placed in the Bible. Construction papers folded and cut, some with sweet sentiments not completely spelled correctly: "Thank you Mother for being *realy* nice." Lace-trimmed cards with glued-on hearts. Theresa's heartfelt note to say thank you for all you had done to help her when her husband left her to raise two teenagers. Sandi's wedding invitation placed to remind us all that *"love is patient; love is kind."* Nestled inside the pages were two stories. Of course, "Ozark Pioneers"! The other story was one I had written at the age of twenty-eight, just prior to my mother's death. It was an assignment about a difficult time in your life, and you had to use stream of consciousness to tell the story. "Face-to-Face" describes the most debilitating situation I had been in during my life, up until the years of grief.

Face to Face

"Her family can't see her like this! Just look at her! She lost a lot of blood during surgery—we need to clean her up—her clothes and hair! Change that pillow case—it's saturated too!" *Was he shouting at me? Um, um, yeah ... oh, my! No? He, was yelling about, me?* Vaguely, I can recall the white and green uniforms hovering over me, like a watercolor photograph, just fading away with too much water—a drowning image. Visions all becoming a blur, but I vividly remember the pain.

On the top of my left hand an I.V. needle pierced its life supporting nutrients throughout my blood stream. A tube which was larger than my nostril was jammed into my sinuses and rammed down my throat where it stopped its traveling. The resting place was my empty stomach. Blood was being irrigated with the use of water. First, the surgical basting instrument shot out the liquid as it rushed through my nose, trickled down the pathway to my stomach. Blood and water were then forced to flush out of my system and I was submissive and could not fight back. Covering what remained of my nose and mouth was an oxygen mask, except for the small tubing sticking out of the corner of my mouth. This straw-like equipment was designed to vacuum the blood from my mouth. Wire loops and stainless steel screws were all that held my jaw together. I had just undergone reconstructive surgery for my severe TMJ (temporomandibular joint) disorder.

In just a mere three hours I was to have a cure for my endless headaches. My prayers would be answered. Clicking and popping in my jaw joints when I yawned or ate would finally cease. No longer would I feel like a cow—the process of chew, chew, chew, just to be sure I could swallow my food. My inch and a half under bite would be terminated for good. Sixteen. Sixteen was the magic number. Sixteen meant the final growth of my jaw. Finally, I had turned the age, sixteen. Poor Pinocchio, I could empathize; he had his nose and I had my jaw.

Reluctantly, she propped the mirror up for me and she continuously watched my failed attempts to grasp the handle with my trembling hands. Next to me, the intensive care nurse was busy adjusting my oxygen mask, EKG, and I.V. bags. "May I please look at my face?" I begged through clenched teeth and shifting jaws. Wow! Behind the mummy-like bandage which was so tightly woven and surrounding my whole head, I could see my nose was swollen more than twice its size, my eyes resembled raccoons, but still I could visualize my new face. My jawline would be perfect—just like everyone else's. Just plain normal. Beyond the cracked and bleeding lips from surgery, I knew that one day, there would be a smile, one with every tooth aligned—side-by-side.

"Are you okay? Cindy, are you alright?" Questioned the nurse, shaking me and sitting at my side in the ICU that night. "You fainted earlier and stopped breathing. We had quite a scare. What you now feel on your neck is an incision we had to make for a breathing tube to be placed. Your chest may feel sore from the compression we had to …" I simply nodded my head to signal I could hear her as I slipped into the dark once again.

Trying to capture that plastic beach ball, I was running as fast as I could. Yellow, blue, green, red, yellow, blue, green, red, yellow, blue, green, red were in a vortex. With awkward steps, I was finally close enough to reach my toy. Instead of retrieving the ball, my little sandals sent those colors rolling again. Like a video camera on instant replay, I acted my part in chasing my plastic companion. Right before the recovering scene, I heard a faint sound, a voice I knew well. "Cindy, look out!" Just for a moment I turned to respond, tripped instead over the crack in the sidewalk; my mouth being the first part of my body to greet the concrete curbing.

"Hey, turn on *I Love Lucy*," I lisped to my parents as I regained consciousness in the hospital room. I had lived through surgery; now my life would change. Nearly all my baby teeth had to be extracted from the roof of my mouth. Somehow, I did feel different, but with my parents nearby, I was only concerned with giggling at Lucy. Yes, there was something different about me, but what?

"Look at Cindy, she looks like that donkey on Hee-Haw, with her missing, spaced teeth," whispered Tonya, to another girl in my fourth grade class, who I just spent recess trying to befriend by sharing my Barbie's clothing with her.

"No she doesn't. I think she looks more like that witch off the Wizard of Oz. You know, the one with the big chin that sticks out," cackled Emily. Thank God they couldn't hear inside my heart or feel the blood pounding and surging through me or see the lumps in my throat forming as I held back the tears. I needed no other reason to be made fun of today, after all.

"Emma and Tonya, please stop this nonsense chattering. I am trying to teach class." Mrs. Larkin was waltzing to the board, her hair was the color of harvest wheat and I thought it danced from shoulder to shoulder. How I wanted to be just like her someday because she was pretty, smart and seemed important. With her white chalk she wrote the word, "inanimate" in her cursive handwriting. She placed fancy scroll designs underneath the watchword of the day. "Let's do something fun today. I want each of you to write a story about what you believe an inanimate object goes through in life. Inanimate means something not living, like my shoes. What do you think my shoes would say if they could talk?" Our lesson went on and I contemplated hard on my pencil in my sweaty hand.

If I Were a Pencil

By Cindy McIntyre
Mrs. Larkin's 4th grade class

I'm always getting lost. Sometimes I get ground up to nothing and then get thrown away. How would you feel? I just sit and wait for someone to come. Sometime I even hope and pray for someone to come. When people get me they put their hot hands all over me until I sweat to death. Then, I wish I could get thrown away or ground up.

I hope someday people will stop doing things to kill me. One time I had to go to the hospital because someone broke my leg and shaved my head too close. I had to have a full body cast. Can you guess how long I was in there? For five whole months! I'm in trouble again.

Oh no! Help! Here comes someone! There's a good place up there on that secret shelf in the closet. If there were only a way I could hide. There's some boxes over there. I'll just stack them up. Then I'll be safe. Oh, it's just a nice old lady. Maybe she'll be good to me. I've always heard of taking a chance. Do you know what I'm doing now? I'm living happily ever after with that nice old lady in her velvet lined pencil box.

Three weeks later our school had an assembly to honor all the classes from kindergarten to senior year. Each grade had either an art project or a story they had to enter into the Jaycees contest. Starting with the kindergarten class they made announcements and awarded the students with small prizes. Finally, they reached the 4th grade. "Cindy McIntyre, please come down and receive your awards for your wonderful story, 'If I Were a Pencil,' blared the principal through his microphone. His voice astounded me and echoed vibrations through me. I felt like I was floating in slow motion while plowing through the legs of the students, sitting in the bleachers. My limbs were numb until I caressed the silkiness of my earned ribbon. In my other hand, I held up my $2.00 bill winnings and shared a proud, toothless grin with the crowd. I welcomed their applause. This was much different than their ridicule. In that particular moment, it was okay to be "Hee-Haw's donkey," or "Oz's" witch, besides they were famous and today I was famous too!

Now, I stand before the mirror reflecting the innocent two-and-a-half-year-old, the downtrodden fourth grade pupil, the hopeful sixteen-year-old, and the twenty-eight-year-old woman. Enveloping them all inside my heart, I sense every trial of pain and laughter. Each person represented has a unique story overflowing with character. This image equals more than a superficial face.

Mom, you stored this essay inside the Bible, and it would be the last one you will save for me. In just one short year, you will be gone. My stories will remain inside the Bible, which I have now inherited. Dad's memorial program will be joining our treasures. It will lie inside the book of John. How were we to condense his ninety years of life?

12

Eulogy of Worth

And ye now therefore have sorrow: but I will see you again, and your heart shall rejoice, and your joy no man taketh from you.
—John 16:22 (KJV)

John William McIntyre, son of Earl and Margaret Parker McIntyre, was born November 21, 1926, in Ottawa, Illinois. He departed this life Sunday, February 12, 2017, in his home, near Lebanon, Missouri, at the age of ninety years, two months, and twenty-one days.

On August 22, 1951, he was united in marriage to Nellie Jeanette Sluder, and to this union three daughters and one son were born.

He was preceded in death by his parents; his wife, Nellie, on December 8, 1999; a granddaughter, Lori Butts; three brothers, Orville, Athel, and Melvin McIntyre; and two sisters, Agatha Bennett and Louise Rossness.

John is survived by three daughters, Sandra Martin, and

her husband, Larry, Theresa Lay, and her husband, Paul, and Cindy McIntyre, and her significant other, James Tucker, all of Lebanon, Missouri; a son, John William "Jay" McIntyre, and his wife, Mary, of Marseilles, Illinois; four grandchildren, Lisa Butts, Doug Butts, Jayson McIntyre, and Kelsey Martin; three great-grandchildren, Lauren Finnell, Dakota Butts, and Bria Finnell; two great-great-grandchildren, Jayden Finnell, and Braxtyn Davis; a number of nieces and nephews; as well as a host of other relatives and friends.

He was born and raised in the Ottawa, Illinois area. John used to talk about living through the depression years and knew what it was like to be hungry and would sacrifice to provide for others. After he and Nellie were married, they made their home in Earlville, Illinois, and John worked for Marathon Electric Corporation. The family moved to Lebanon, Missouri, in 1981, and John continued to work for Marathon Electric compiling over thirty years of service to the corporation.

John was saved and baptized at a young age and maintained his Christian faith throughout the years.

He enjoyed summers the most. He was able to spend time with Cindy shopping, eating out, and searching far and wide for the best tasting tomatoes. He greatly enjoyed visiting the animal shelter during their outings and dearly loved animals. He adopted "Boots" the cat after Nellie passed away, and when Boots left this world, he welcomed a new cat, "Peanut," into his home.

He also enjoyed coin and stamp collecting. He was a

consummate storyteller and always had a joke for every occasion. He possessed a delightful sense of humor, was fiercely independent, and liked to laugh. He had recently become a fan of *The Walking Dead* television show, and in his last days enjoyed binge-watching the series. His family was very important to him, and he especially enjoyed all his grandchildren.

John was a loving father, grandfather, great-grandfather, great-great-grandfather, and uncle, and was a kind and caring neighbor and friend. John had a special way of saying goodbye, and so we suggest today that in saying farewell to John use his favorite saying, "I love you, and God does too."

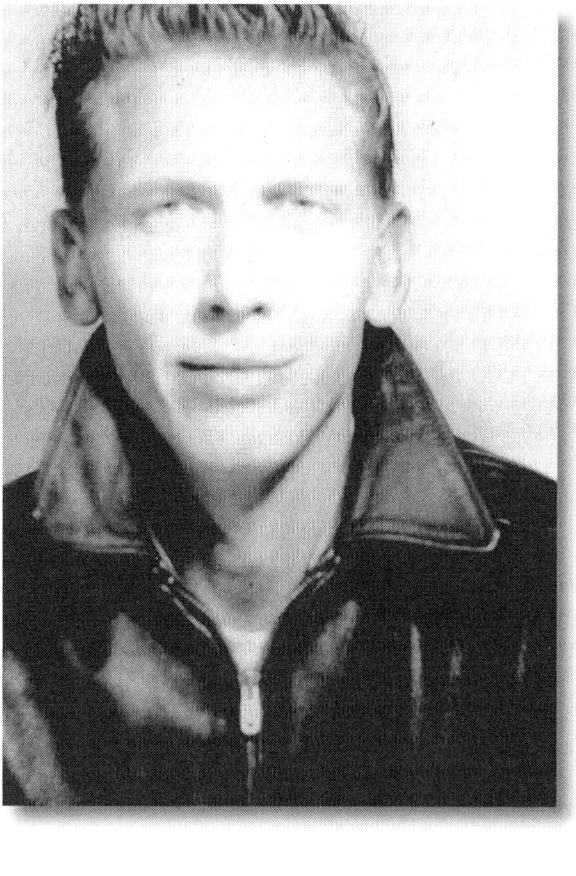

13

GRIEF UNSCRIPTED

> He healeth the broken in heart, and bindeth up their wounds.
> —Psalm 147:3 (KJV)

Dear Mom,

You likely know, but I just lost Dad. You were reunited with him for Valentine's Day, 2017. My heart is broken all over again. Now, it's a combined hurt of rehashing your loss along with his. I tried so hard to take good care of him. He became my new routine when you were gone. We shopped together, dined out (KFC, Captain D's, and Mexican restaurants for taco salads), and went on spins to nowhere. Well, maybe these journeys ended with him finding tomatoes. There are so many stories to tell. Forty-seven years' worth. That's what I almost was given as far as the number of years with him—same as you, Mom. Both of you are characters full of life whose stories could fill the pages of a book, and that's exactly

what I intend to do. Thank you for leaving behind the lyrics of songs inside your purse, your journal filled with the hurts you experienced as child, and for giving me life, even when I thought I wasn't wanted. Yes, there's a story to tell here. You are more than trinkets inside a lock box; more than just black-and-white photos hidden inside the pages of an album.
Dear Mom & Dad,

I miss you both so dearly. Dad, I miss you most when school lets out and it's our time to go for a spin. Tomatoes were on sale the other day, $.88 a pound. Holding back tears, I walked on, but I almost had to leave the store because it just didn't feel right not loading up the cart with them. KFC sure looks lonely too. They have a new sauce I want to try, but you're not here to go. Wishing you were here with me, eating and enjoying your chicken breast, smashed potatoes, and biscuits. Also, I cannot seem to build up enough courage to go back into *our* grocery store, where I purchased chicken breasts from the deli, so many of them, in fact, they put them all inside a box that I called "the pet carrier."

    Mom, Dad claimed he would have considered going into senior housing, but he wanted to wait until "later in life." He was only eight-nine-years old at the time. Mom and Dad, please tell me somehow that I did right by allowing Dad to live independently in my home. Please let my heart be at more peace and stop blaming myself for not doing more.

    Dad, I am now so aware of just how deep an impact your life made on me. Watching you and Mom as I grew up taught me by example how a man should treat others. I have discovered your love notes and cards to Mom. One in particular you wrote, "You and the children mean the whole world to me. I thank God for all of you." I remember you hiding Mom's famous paisley green nightgown behind the giant console TV. You were planning to surprise her with it on Valentine's Day, over twenty years ago. Your example, as a kindhearted man, made me picky, and for that I have so much gratitude. Now, I can be selective and not settle. Dad, I am grateful you had the opportunity to build a relationship with James. Having your blessing on loving him helped me confirm my choice and provided me assurance. Although you will never physically walk me down the aisle in my wedding, I will always remember that you and I walked hand-in-hand and heart-to-heart throughout nearly forty-seven years of my life, even as our roles as parent and child shifted.

Dad, I knew you were growing tired. Your wishes had always been to remain at home as long as possible and not suffer inside a nursing home with no quality of life. Please know I did all I could to help you and honor each of your wishes. You died peacefully at home, in your sleep.

I will miss starting at one end of town and making my way down Jefferson Street, pulling first into Captain D's, ordering your fish and chicken dinner, being instructed, "Take out the hushpuppies for yourself." Then, stopping at Wendy's for a couple cheeseburgers. Chinese would be the next destination, where you would be wanting cashew chicken, and I knew to remove the crab rangoon because you weren't eating them. You'd be saying, "Add those crab raccoons to those hushpuppies because I'm not about to eat either of them." Little Caesar's pizza was also on the menu. Running inside, as you were watching me from the car. Once, you said, "Got a bit concerned and that's the only reason I was honking the horn at you. I couldn't see you standing in line." Our fast food journey is almost complete, but not without an extra crispy chicken breast dinner from KFC. Splurging on these once-a-month treats was your routine. You'd laugh when I went to drop you off and say, "You can have the weekend free now. I think I'll have plenty to eat!" By the next week, you would be telling me, "I am so shaky and sick at my guts. I'm hurting like a dog who has been trying to pass a peach seed!" Yet, off you wanted to go for a ride.

Mistakenly, I still reach for the phone to call you. It doesn't feel right not to see you or talk to you each and every day. You always provided me with tons of stories to share. I miss you claiming, "Hey, I've got something to show you; hey, I've got something to tell you; hey, I've got something to give you." Adventures always awaited me; I just never knew what to do to prepare myself for what I might see, hear, and find. I miss pulling into your driveway and seeing you, waiting impatiently for me, peeking out from the picture window—you were so sweet and childlike.

Recently, I had a dream that you were standing between Mom and me. She and I were each holding one of your hands. As a trio, we were walking across a bridge. No words

Eulogies Unspoken

were ever spoken. My hand grasped yours so tight because I was never going to be ready to say good-bye. Letting go of your hand and allowing Mom to lead you on was both burdensome and joyful. After all, you were on your way to the streets of gold with her. Perhaps you are together walking in those beautiful gardens that Mom wrote about. Upon waking, I wipe the tears away while I reminiscence her singing, "Across the bridge, there's no more sorrow; across the bridge, there's no more pain."

Both rejoicing and mourning have me so emotionally tangled. You were my buddy who was primed and ready and was supposed to live to see one hundred. Dad, you gave me almost forty-seven years of love, same as you gave Mom. Dad, was the love I gave you in return enough?

14

Unexpected Halos

> Be not forgetful to entertain strangers: for thereby some have entertained angels unawares.
> —Hebrews 13:2 (KJV)

Imposter? Can anyone get a read on the real me, a full sense of my whole character? Because I am the composition of a million tiny stories comprised of John and Nellie McIntyre. Forty-seven chapters of life, to be exact. Grief has been organizing a timeline for me. Indexing, measuring, and marking the contents of time with dog-eared pages: writing my story, *Face-to-Face*, one year before my mom died; buying my Ford car six months before my mom died; earning my master's degree four months before my mom died; becoming my father's primary caregiver the very moment my mom died; journaling Dear Mom letters, beginning just one month after my mom died; attempting to celebrate my thirtieth birthday seven months after my mom died; accepting my current teaching position eight months after my mom died;

certifying in secondary social studies one year after my mom died; purchasing my first home four years after my mom died; meeting James and each of his family members and truly falling in love with each of them eight years after my mom died; letting go of my mom's chocolate Santa ten years after she died; sitting by my mother's engraved headstone during my father's funeral eighteen years after she died; unknowingly writing the very first words of this book as a journal of healing eighteen years ago, just after my mom died; continuing to uncover treasure after treasure every day since my dad died.

Donating most my father's clothing to Goodwill seemed the appropriate protocol. Passing on his favorite polo shirts in the various approved three shades of blue, green, and browns, I hoped would benefit someone is need. Tags were still attached to the sweater Sandi had purchased for him at Christmas. His plan was to save it to wear to his next doctor's appointment coming up, so he would appear presentable. Each article of clothing I touched and examined had a story, which I visited in my mind. James had recently found Dad the snap-front shirts he loved and often wore, since buttons had become a bit of a challenge. My mind's eye began created to-do lists and establishing priorities of all the chores still left to accomplish. Hadn't I just recently washed, dried, folded, and placed these socks, undershirts, and pants inside these very dresser drawers? This was their home, where they belonged.

Grabbing the handles of the dresser, I wanted to slam

and open and slam and open the dresser's emptying drawers. Thankfully, some oddities made me chipper. Dad had placed a few cough drop wrappers and their fragments inside the corner of the top dresser drawer. He must have been saving them for later. The top drawer was a place for his odds and ends and some collectables. Nearby, Theresa and Sandi begin sorting through the nightstand, providing us a moment to pause and laugh at the half-eaten tomato sandwich inside. Then I remember he's gone—having died in his sleep, just a foot away, in that king-sized bed, where we found him.

Deep dresser drawers, five in all, were now empty. Even my favorite drawer with the three dividers. It was the perfect drawer when I was young, and I claimed it with a blue crayon and my byline: *McIntyre, 4,* with such gratification that I could spell my name. Dad said, "We capitalize the 'I' because we are Irish!" So I memorized that lesson and vowed I would not forget, putting it all to the test that day, succeeding. Plus, I could write my numbers and enjoyed my signature, attached with my age. Authorship of that dresser had been set in place. However, the crayon marks have since faded and the entire contents of this magical piece of furniture now vacant. What were we even going to do with this dresser and its matching mirrored top console? Looking into the mirror, I can see the blank expression on my face, pondering that very question. I had promised to rent my father's house to Kelsey, my niece, and in just a few days, she would be moving in.

Stored inside my garage, the furniture sat, awaiting a

decision. Rain was forecasted for days, and my mood was just as stormy. Displaced—both me and that furniture. Although I had not been kicked out of my dad's home, it resonated in that fashion. This location is where I was expected to show up every day after work. Where would I go now? Who would be expecting me? When would I find a buyer or just the right person in which to make a furniture donation?

Kelsey reluctantly shared the news with me: the mirrored console dresser had become loose and cracked, breaking the upper left-hand side of the piece. Grief set in again, over the loss of a mirror. Suddenly, it became my family's heirloom. It wasn't the first time this mirror was broken. Theresa used this mirror as a vanity, leaning way in to learn the correct way to apply her makeup. She always wanted to keep up with trends by staying real *groovy*. One day, her lean-in turned more into a sit-in, and it cracked. But this was a time when life was fixable. Both our parents were alive, and we could count on them to solve life's broken issues.

Now, I am broken over shattered glass and an overwhelming fear that something else is going to occur. Decision finally made: I had to have that furniture for myself. No one else was going to protect it like I would. Arranging my office furniture around, it seemed I had enough space, after all, to make the two pieces fit perfectly. Lisa, my friend, who I hadn't visited with in years, appeared in person to listen and guide me. During times of grief, those friends who give of their time and prayers are like angels. Helping those so lost and brokenhearted in just the simplest of ways reverberates out into the universe and lets the healing process begin. Praying for myself through grief's daily trials seemed fruitless. I had many people praying for me—family, friends, co-workers, and church members. Unaware, I had James and his father watching the weather radar on my behalf and arranging a time to pick up the dressers for me—carefully dodging rainstorms. A mass of emotions ranging from A to Z, anger to zeal, flowed through me during this whole ordeal.

Lisa took me to my dad's garage, grabbed a broom, and swept up the broken glass for me. Very ironic that cleaning up the shards of glass seemed symbolic of my own brokenness being mended, piece by piece. James and his father also came through for me. Those two dressers arrived without further damages.

Once alone, I sat on the floor, next to tall dresser, allowing myself the chance to grieve the loss of forty-seven years' worth of memories contained in the magical dresser with the five deep drawers and the three dividers. Still a child at heart, I was McIntyre, 4—flustered, orphaned, and paralyzed with grief.

Draping a scarf over the corner of the broken mirror, I hide the damage so well that no one would even know; I've become a pro at hiding damages, especially in myself, with an outward smile. Two of the large family Bibles, stuffed with loving treasures, found a home on the dresser with the mirrored shelf. Also reflected in the mirror is a gift my dad bought my mom: a white dove musical box which plays the love song, "You Light up My Life." I give it a twist often to hear the tune. A nearby trinket box contains my father's watch; although it no longer keeps time, its value is eternal.

Like my mother so many years ago, I still longed for peace in my soul after the passing of my own father. Not because I wasn't sure if he was a Christian and was in heaven, but because I wasn't sure about my own faith. God had taken away from me, again. I felt defeated. What do you want from me, God? What direction are you taking me in on this tailspin of grief? What great plan can come of all this hurt? Question after question, I begged God to answer me: show me a sign, give me hope that I can get through this grief and find a positive outlet for it to help others.

I began to dust out and vacuum each of the deep drawers of the dresser. They were still completely empty, but I planned to turn them into a creativity center to store crafts, along with family photos for scrapbooking. On the top, I displayed my favorite photo, a canvas print of my mom and dad which Lisa had given me. My mother's photograph, which always evokes "You look just like your mother," is prominent, as a constant reminder of her faith and love. Dad is in his leather jacket, looking so young, in black and white. My dusting, vacuuming, and sorting continues. One by one, I add sentimental items to the top drawer.

Dad's prized stamp collection and his brand new box of pencils, all nestle into place. Smirking, I remember my story, *If I Were a Pencil*, and I contemplate that if I, indeed, were a pencil, there is no other place I would rather be, because this dresser is home. Viewing my dad's photo, I also begin considering the notion of tenderly holding one of those pencils in my hand to begin writing the story of our eighteen years of adventures together, while I served as his caregiver. I work down to my favorite drawer, the one I proudly signed McIntyre, cognizant of the fact I had placed a claim on this very dresser, since the age of four. Slowly, the overflowing drawers begin to bring a bit of fulfillment.

Wedged into the corner of the drawer, in divider number one, a broken snap or button is stuck. Administering all my strength, I attempted to pry it out, but it just will not budge. Persevering with my fingernails, I dig and dig until I could see it was actually something golden. Funny, no one saw this while emptying out the drawer, and it didn't fall out during the move? Or I hadn't noticed it before while helping Dad put away his clothes, over the years. Grabbing the vacuum, once again, I go after it. I still have zero luck removing this annoying thing. Sighing, I mentally shout, *Fine; forget it.*

Walking away, I begin wallowing in self-pity: "Why me, God? Have you figured out a purpose for me, other than more suffering? Can I beg for a little mercy on my soul?"

Pacing the floor in circles, I stare at the mess I have created with my mom and dad's belongings, in various piles to be sorted. Picking up random items, such as my dad's coffee pot and my mom's bird figurines, I'm wondering where I will locate them or what's next in my life. Nothing seems to make a bit of sense to me. At least I am a pro in the arena of distress. Grief-stricken again, I pile myself into the fetal position on the couch and let the tears flow. One minute, I am reminded of the visual image of finding my father's lifeless body, and in the next minute, I am attempting to calm myself with the fact that he is now with my mother, and they are at peace together. Up and then down, the emotional elevator known as grief. It's tormenting. It's torturous. It's the ultimate Catch-22. There's no right answer to be found. Eventually, the elevator stops at the floor of relief, where I mull over this fact: *I am lucky.* I had two parents who loved me. Of course, it was okay for me to long for them and for me to occasionally slip into moments of childish behaviors, because they are the main characters in the story of my life. They are worthy of being missed.

"Mother, how many Bibles does one need?" I tease her often, in my mind. Back in the office, I investigate the answer to my question because I can see her personalized Bible, with its bookmark, *Praise God*, poking out. "Nellie McIntyre" is inscribed in gold lettering on the bottom right-hand side of the maroon leather. Two giant family Bibles, both filling the pages with our family treasures, are stacked beneath. Likely, there are more I will uncover. Should I become fortunate enough for this to occur, I will graciously add them as part of a growing collection and consider each of them earthly riches I have acquired. I think of how indebted I am to my parents, especially my mother, who raised me in a Christian home—beginning in Earlville, Illinois. Just on the edge of town, nestled among the corn fields was our country church. *Friendly Welcome*, the perfect name for a humble church, inside a quaint town. Here is where I first listened to my mom's many songs of testimony. Hymns of faith, hope, and prayer are engraved in my heart. Today, I can walk into church and sing those very same hymns, without needing a songbook.

Onward: That was the direction I needed to go. Removing the item that remained stuck required at least one final effort on my part. Knowingly, I braced myself for the chore. Determining the words my mother might say to me about this dilemma, I get an earful, in my mind: *Can't you just be calm and have a little faith?*

Millimeter by millimeter, I tugged on the shiny item jammed inside. Triangle of gold? Wiggling and wiggling, back and forth, bits more appear. What button, snap, or tack would be in a shape such as this? Enough of the triangle eventually surfaced, and I gave it a hefty hank. Flying out was a shiny little item. Holding it inside the palm of my hand, I was awestruck. Unexpected halos: In my sight was a pin with the enchanting face of a tiny, golden angel. With her praying hands and her eyes shut, she still looked up at me, with a smile as if to say, "Remember me?" Her triangular wing had been buried deep inside that dresser drawer. Unable to fly, for eighteen years. Yet I had an inkling this heavenly object was watching my dad and me—guiding, protecting, and loving us. Since Dad no longer needed her presence here on earth, she stayed in hiding, just waiting. Awaiting for eighteen years. Awaiting the perfect moment to emerge. Awaiting for me. God's little messenger appeared to me in one of my darkest hours, delivering me the blessings of hope, peace, and faith—all I needed.

Acknowledgments

There are so many people who deserve my thanks.

James Tucker—to the one who loves me through the toughest days, always giving me what I need, whether it's support or space. Your help with Dad was precious. Love you always, because that's the plan.

My sister, Theresa Lay (Paul)—to the one who seems most proud and excited about this book. I love and appreciate you. Thanks for becoming a big fan.

My sister, Sandi "Princess" Martin (Larry)—to the one who assured me that my book would not embarrass her. I love you. You get me. Thanks for giving Dad's cat Peanut a loving home.

My brother, John Jay—to the oldest sibling, who lives too far away. You are still a big part of the story. Love you.

My niece, Kelsey Martin—to my "daughter," who spent many childhood days with me. I love you but can't believe you "kicked" me out of my house.

My Aunt Joan Bakken—to the one who was available by phone and allowed me to vent, in the earliest stages of my grief.

Lisa Jones—to the one who brought me lemon cake (great icing) and spent time just listening. Plus, you were one of the biggest proofreaders. Your friendship means so much.

Jackie Jones—to the one who will always be my "Hardly-Able Sister."

Janet Branch—to the one who has been a dear friend and co-worker to me for years; you gave me so much encouragement to keep moving forward with this project.

Regina Esther—to the one who made me first consider publishing this book. Your words of encouragement gave me the driving force. Your prayers and belief in me mean so much.

Donna Pfannenstiel—to the one who provides me some comic relief yet also says so many prayers for me and assures me that my parents would be proud.

Kassie, Lesli, and Sara—to the girls from work who read portions of the book in its earliest stages. It's a blessing to work with each member at HEC.

Doug and Lisa Butts—to my favorite pioneers

Ally and Kat Tucker—to my supportive "daughters," whom I love and am grateful to have in my life.

My students—to those who have stories of adversity, much like my parents: You inspire me.

My teachers—to those of you who fostered my writing over the years; I promised a handful of you that I would never forget your impact.

Tucker/Lawrence clan—to those of you who took in

this grieving "orphan" and gave her a welcoming extended family. Anna, thanks for all the support via text.

Lee Todd and Concord Christian Church—to all of you for your support and prayers

Final Note

Dear Readers,

Thank you for reading my book. It's very likely that you and I share something in common: a love for family or you, too, may be struggling with grief. That was my whole driving force for writing my first book. I wanted to share my stories with others as a way to heal. Grief is such a tricky issue. Some days, you are up, and other days, you are so debilitated. Hopefully, some of the experiences I wrote about, you can see within yourself: anger, child-like moments, and days of wavering with faith.

My book actually started as a personal journal after my mom died. My Dear Mom letters are honest and raw. Writing has always been a coping mechanism for me; it's cathartic. My mission or true goal in writing this book was to share my family's stories in hopes that others might find something within the pages that might comfort them. It helps knowing we are not alone. Passing on our deepest hurts can have a profound healing effect. I plan to reach out to those in grief groups and help them learn to journal their way through the process.

I was also a caregiver to my dad for many years. There are so many stories left within me to share.

Made in the USA
Coppell, TX
13 February 2023

12710914R00067